For my family.
and friends, who are like family.

G.H x

For my Gang-Gang.
One of the greatest role models
I've ever known.

I love you.

CL x

Gordon Woodwards
1930-2022

Gemma Hunt's
SEE! LET'S BE
Me

illustrated by Charlotte Cooke

LION
Children's Books

Published by **Lion Children's Books**
www.spckpublishing.co.uk
Part of the SPCK Group
SPCK, Studio 101, The Record Hall,
16–16A Baldwins Gardens, London, EC1N 7RJ

ISBN 978-0-7459-9806-0

First edition 2023

A catalogue record for this book is available from the British Library

Produced on paper from sustainable sources

First printed by Dream Colour (Hong Kong) Printing Ltd.

Contents

Keep Trying

Shoes! They come in all different shapes and sizes. Some are for running, some are for dancing. Some are for wearing around the house to keep cosy, or at the beach where it's sandy, or jumping in puddles when it's rainy.

But, why do I need to wear shoes with **LACES**? They're so tricky to tie. Cross them over and tuck under. Make bunny ears and cross over and in the hole. Where's the bunny hole?!

Now I'm CONFUSED *and my laces are all in a knot.*
Maybe I should just hide them or lose them,
then I won't have to wear them!
But losing things isn't **fun**.

I was **playing** with Mummy's jewellery box when one of her important rings fell on the floor and **bounced** away.

Keep Trying

I looked for it under the bed, behind the dressing table and under the rug. Mummy **shook** out the duvet, looked in the pillow cases, and under the sheets. We **didn't** give up.

Keep Trying

I turned on the lights, looked under clothes, and **wiggled** the curtains. Mummy moved books and emptied out boxes. But we couldn't find it and Mummy looked **sad**.

I helped Mummy to look **all** around her bedroom. I even went to the hallway to see if it had **rolled** along to my room. Mummy looked, I searched, we shook everything but we couldn't find her ring.

Keep Trying

we **HAD** to
keep looking.

Keep Trying

I sighed and looked at my shoes, the ones with the laces, and was just about to move them, when I saw **something**. The ring was on the shoe! It was sitting on my lace, sparkling in the sunlight, looking so **bright** and happy to be found.

Mummy was so pleased, she **hugged** me and kissed me and ran to tell Daddy. She phoned Nanna and sent a message to Granddad to ask them to join us at the pizza restaurant to **celebrate**.

Keep Trying

Mummy wore a lovely dress and her ring looked so beautiful and sparkly. I really wanted to look smart too, so I took my shoes with laces and carefully crossed the laces.

I tucked one underneath, made two **bunny ears** and sent one in the rabbit hole, pulled them tight and **MADE A BOW**. I did it, I tied my laces! I kept going. I didn't give up, just like Mummy, and now we look and feel great!

Feeling Cross

This is my favourite night in the month. My little sister
and I are having a **sleepover** at Nanna's house!
We both pack our bags with our favourite pyjamas,
fluffy socks, and a cosy blanket. My sister packs her
snuggly toy, Babbit, and I take my turtle called Shelly.
It's going to be so much fun! We'll make **popcorn**,
watch a movie, and snuggle up on the sofa before
going to our beds. Then, in the morning, Nanna will
make pancakes drizzled in syrup with fruit faces.
I love the banana and blueberry eyes. I can't wait.
It's going to be perfect!

Dad dropped us off at Nanna's house and my sister **rushed** upstairs to the bedroom. I kicked off my shoes, threw my things on the floor, and went to turn the TV on to choose a movie.

Feeling Cross

Feeling Cross

Nanna brought in the popcorn and snacks, and my sister joined us in her pyjamas with her blanket and Babbit. It was **so special**, we had such a nice time, until we went to bed.

Feeling Cross

As we walked upstairs, my sister ran past and jumped into the green spotty bed. The green spotty bed that **I ALWAYS** sleep in, next to her purple stripy bed.

"What are you doing?" I shouted.
"That's **MY** bed. Get out, get out now!"

Feeling Cross

I was so cross that I pulled the end of the duvet off the bed and **snatched** it away. My sister started to cry as Nanna came in and asked, "What is going on here?"

I **shouted**, "She's in my bed, Nanna. I sleep in this bed and she's already in it and she needs to get out!"

Nanna **calmly** said, "My love, I can see you are very cross that she has taken your bed, but don't you think you should look at what you have done this evening?

"You walked in the house, **threw** your things in the middle of the hallway for us to stumble over and haven't picked them up or changed into your pyjamas. Don't you think you should sort yourself out before you worry about your sister?"

Feeling Cross

I frowned and **slammed** the door and ran downstairs to get my bag. I felt so hot and sick in my **tummy**, but I knew that Nanna was right.

Feeling Cross

Nanna came and sat next to me on the bottom of the stairs to help me calm down. "Don't be **angry** so easily. Anger will not help you live a good life. You're quick to point out what your sister has done wrong, but you need to also look at the bad things you have done too. So, take a deep breath and pick up your things. I'll come and tuck you both in."

I helped Nanna make the bed again. I **hugged** my sister and said sorry because I didn't want to go to sleep feeling cross. She gave me a kiss and let me sleep with the green pillow, which looked great next to Shelly. I can't **wait** for the morning, I'm going to make a rabbit face on my sister's pancake!

Bring Joy

OUCH! I bashed my toe and it really, really hurts.
OWW! Daddy you're pulling on my hair with the brush.
OWW again! The hair band is too tight. **AAARGH!**

My clothes are too itchy. **URGH!** My cereal is too soggy.
EWWW, the toothpaste is too spicy. **DADDY!** I'm
bored. I don't have anything to do. **AAAHH!**

Dad whispered "Come on. This doesn't sound like our
happy, joyful girl. Who is this grumpy, moany girl?"

"Where's my **smiley** girl who is happy eating cereal from the packet, twirling around in fancy dress and singing really loudly?

Bring Joy

"You love to sing along to **anything** - nursery rhymes, pop songs, TV jingles and Christmas carols. You sing Christmas songs **ALL** through the year! I heard you singing 'Joy to the world' last night when Mummy asked you to clear the dinner table.

Bring Joy

"You sounded like an angel, just like the angel Gabriel you dressed up as in the school nativity.

Come and **look** at this photo.

"Do you remember how **YOU** brought the exciting news of joy and happiness to everyone? As the angel Gabriel, you said that Mary was going to have the special baby named Jesus.

"Jesus would be the **super star** of the world and Gabriel was the first one to get excited about this. What great news to be happy about!

Bring Joy

"The angel wasn't **moaning** or **grumpy**. If Gabriel had been, we might not have known about the first Christmas, which really brings joy to the world!"

Daddy gave me the photo and went downstairs. I looked at the picture and quietly sang "Joy to the world..." as Mummy came out of the bedroom with a **HUGE** smile on her face and a big thumbs up.

OOHH! I knew what that meant. There was good news to tell. We ran downstairs and I told everyone. "Mummy has got the new job! Yeah! Mummy, we are so excited for you!"

AHHH, that felt good to share something fun and joyful. I might just find my angel costume and put it on again!

Finding Peace

My sister is having a play date with friends today. They are dressing up, building castles with blocks, and **squashing** animal shapes into modelling clay while mooing and baaing loudly. Mum is baking some cakes and the whisk keeps **whizzing**. Dad is cutting the grass and the lawn mower is really roaring.

Nanna is helping to cut back trees, her saw keeps grinding. Granddad is here too, he's just reading the newspaper. I wanted to finish my sail boat puzzle today but there is too much noise going on and I can't concentrate.

Finding Peace

Moo! Whiz! Roar! AARGH! I can't stand this sound any more, it's making my head hurt. My sister and her friends are all giggling.

I beg them, "Please, play quietly!"

Mum is **crashing** pots and pans together. I shout, "Mum! You're too noisy." But she can't hear me over the noise.

Finding Peace

Finding Peace

Dad is taking **AGES** to cut the grass, making it look all smart in stripes like a green zebra. I scream into the garden, "Dad! Are you nearly finished?" But he can't hear me as Nanna is **sawing** so many branches, like a tree-cutting machine. There will only be a trunk left.

There is just **SO MUCH NOISE!**
And no one will listen to me.

Finding Peace

So, I run to Granddad. "Why aren't you doing anything Granddad? How can you just **sit there** while all this noise is going on around you. Why won't you do **something**?"

I thought my head was going to explode.

Finding Peace

Granddad carefully **folded** up his newspaper, stood up and calmly said, "Come on everyone, be quiet, be still."

And just like that, silence.

The mooing stopped. The whisk went quiet. The mower turned off. I couldn't **believe** it. I had really tried to make the noise stop by shouting at Mum, jumping up and down to get Dad's attention and **screaming** at my sister.

But all I had to do was be calm, like Granddad, to bring peace and quiet to our house. I was just adding to the noise and chaos. I want to be more like Granddad and keep cool, calm, and chilled.

It'll be hard, but I will try to speak calmly next time to keep our home peaceful. That is a much better way for me to be.

Finding Peace

Feeling Jealous

I love the winter. I like the snow and the ice, wearing hats and gloves, and especially I love drinking hot chocolate to keep warm. Each year, our local winter market has a hot chocolate stall that my Granddad runs. He makes the **BEST** hot chocolate with squirty cream, marshmallows, and chocolate sprinkles. The queue for his hot chocolate is always **SO** long that this year Granddad has given us pocket money to help him. My sister says she is too little to help, so she takes her pocket money from Granddad and goes off to look around the market. Why does she get to have fun when I'm working?

The market has music playing, smells of yummy food in the air, and **bright lights** twinkling. As I hand over a mug of hot chocolate, I can see my sister going up and down, around and around on the carousel, squealing with excitement as she shouts, "Giddy up horsie!"

Feeling Jealous

Feeling Jealous

I **squirt** cream on top of the mug and a little goes on my hand as I'm distracted by my sister taking a big stick of candy floss and eating it **ALL** up.

As I wipe the cream off my hand and start to sprinkle marshmallows on the hot chocolate, I notice that my sister now has a long fishing rod and is hooking a duck out of a pond. She hooks out the **BIGGEST** duck and gets given a **HUGE** purple teddy bear as a prize!

Feeling Jealous

I wish I was out there playing, but I need to finish this hot chocolate with Granddad's special ingredient: chocolate sprinkles with gingerbread. I shake the sprinkles on without looking what I'm doing as I **CANNOT** believe that my sister has now spent her money on a delicious burger with cheese, onions, lettuce, and pickles!

Feeling Jealous

As she comes back to our stall, she looks sad as she doesn't have money left for a hot chocolate. Granddad takes the one I've just made and gives it to **HER**!

Feeling Jealous

That's not **fair**! I've been making these for everyone else and not once did I get one for myself, while my sister went and spent all her money at the market.

Feeling Jealous

Granddad brought me over a big mug of his famous hot chocolate and said that I didn't need to be jealous of my sister. I can have all the hot chocolate I want. He said that, now she has come back safely from the market, we can tell her the **secret** family ingredient for our famous hot chocolate. So, I hand my sister the chocolate sprinkles and give her a wink as I show her the gingerbread, which she pours all over my drink.

Feeling Jealous

The stories in this book have been inspired by these Bible stories:

Keep Trying

The parable of the lost coin
Luke 15:8–10

Feeling Cross

Jesus speaks about judging others
Matthew 7:3–5

Bring Joy

The angel Gabriel visits Mary
Luke 1:26—38

Finding Peace

Jesus calms the storm
Mark 4:35–41

Feeling Jealous

The parable of the prodigal son
Luke 15:11–32

"Gemma has done a lovely job of bringing to life
the teachings of Jesus for the everyday experience
of children and their families."

Bob Hartman
Storyteller and award-winning author

Gemma Hunt's
SEE! LET'S BE
A Good Friend

Illustrated by Charlotte Cooke

ALSO AVAILABLE

Gemma Hunt's See! Let's Be
A Good Friend

ISBN 9780745979519